PEOPLE OF THE
PLAINS & PRAIRIES

by
LINDA THOMPSON

ROURKE CLASSROOM RESOURCES
The path to student success
Vero Beach, Florida 32964

www.rourkepublishing.com

PHOTO CREDITS:
Library of Congress, Prints & Photographs Division, Edward S. Curtis Collection: cover, title page, pages 8, 10, 13, 16, 27-29, 31, 32, 35-42; Courtesy of the U.S. Fish & Wildlife Service: pages 3. 4, 6; Courtesy Charles Reasoner: pages 6, 14, 16, 25; Courtesy of The Division of Anthropology, American Museum of Natural History (AMNH): pages 7, 8, 16, 18, 19, 21, 22, 25-27, 30-34, 37, 39, 40, 43; Courtesy of the Burton Historical Collection, Detroit Public Library: page 9; National Portrait Gallery, Smithsonian Institution: pages 10, 14; Western History/Genealogy Department, Denver Public Library: pages 11, 12, 20; National Anthropological Archives, Smithsonian Institution: 12, 14, 17-19, 27, 28, 35, 36, 43; Library of Congress: page 29.

DESIGN AND LAYOUT by Rohm Padilla, Mi Casa Publications, printing@taosnet.com

Library of Congress Cataloging-In-Publication Data

Thompson, Linda, 1941-
 People of the plains and prairies / by Linda Thompson.
     p. cm. -- (Native peoples, Native lands)
Includes bibliographical references and index.
Contents: The plains and prairie people today -- Where they came from --
Life on the plains and prairies -- What they believe.
 ISBN 1-58952-757-7 (hardcover)
 1. Indians of North America--Great Plains--History--Juvenile
literature. 2. Indians of North America--Prairie
Provinces--History--Juvenile literature. 3. Indians of North
America--Great Plains--Social life and customs--Juvenile literature. 4.
Indians of North America--Prairie Provinces--Social life and
customs--Juvenile literature. [1. Indians of North America--Great
Plains. 2. Indians of North America--Prairie Provinces.] I. Title.
II. Series: Thompson, Linda, 1941-   Native peoples, Native lands.
 E78.G73.T715 2003
 971.2004'97--dc21
                              2003011544

Ppk 1-58952-892-1

Printed in the USA

Title Page Image
For strength and visions, Apsaroke man during Sundance Ceremony;
photo by Edward S. Curtis.

TABLE OF CONTENTS

Guadalupe Mountains
National Park, Texas

Chapter I:
PEOPLE OF THE PLAINS & PRAIRIES

*T*he **Plains and Prairie People** are the best known of the various groups of **Native Americans** or **American Indians**. This familiarity comes partly from many movies that have been made about 19th century conflicts between Europeans and Plains tribes, such as the Sioux [soo]. Also, ceremonial **dances**, dress, and rituals from this region are perhaps more familiar than those of other Native groups.

Perhaps 400,000 Plains and Prairie People once occupied this region before Christopher Columbus "discovered" America in 1492. Their homeland was what is now the central United States and parts of Alberta, Saskatchewan, and Manitoba, Canada. This vast region stretched westward from the Mississippi River and contained the present states of North and South Dakota, Nebraska, Kansas, Oklahoma, Arkansas, southern Minnesota, two-thirds of Montana, much of Missouri and Iowa, most of Louisiana, and central Texas.

Arapaho National Wildlife
Refuge in Jackson County,
Colorado

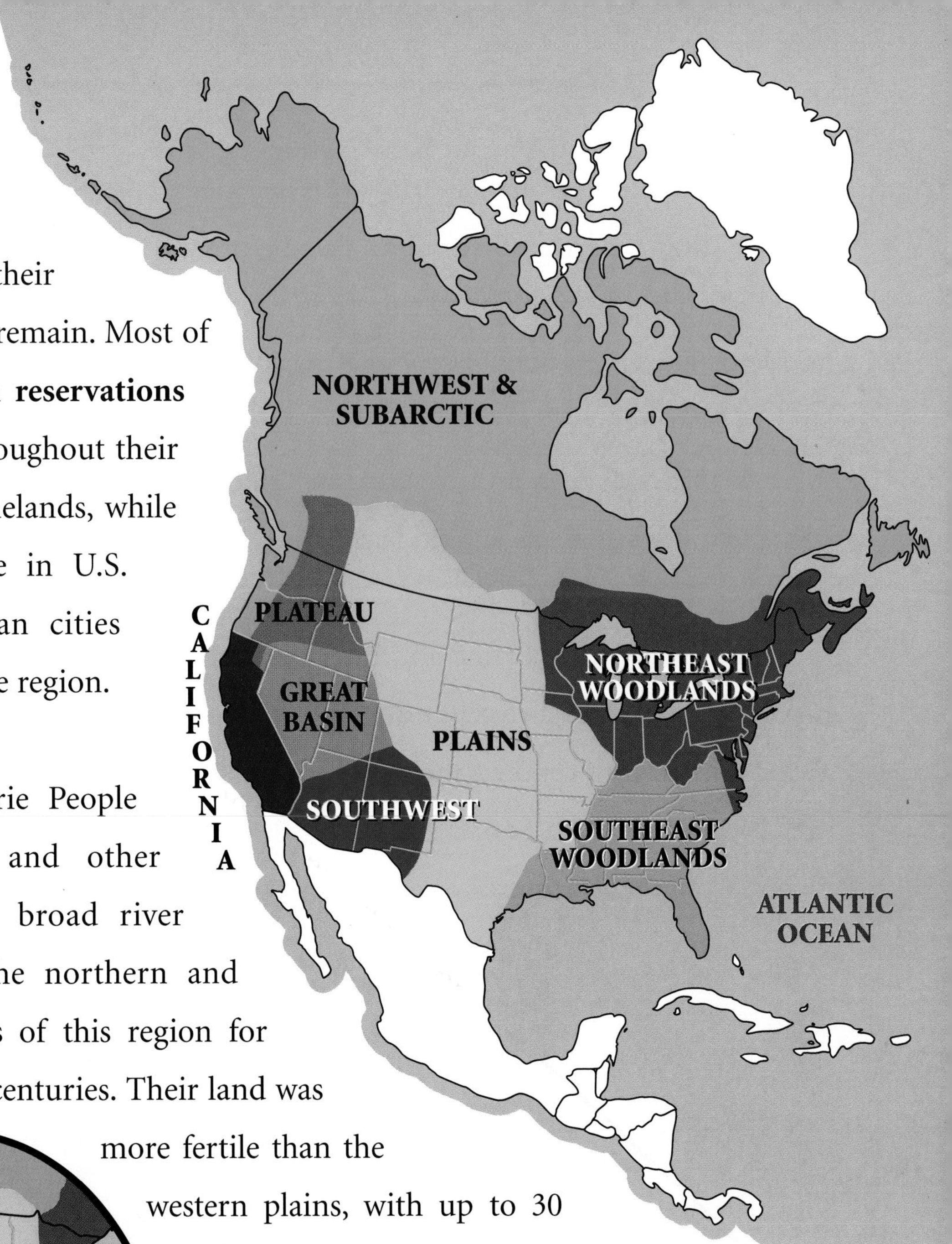

Today, more than 600,000 of their descendants remain. Most of them live on **reservations** scattered throughout their original homelands, while others reside in U.S. and Canadian cities outside of the region.

The Prairie People grew corn and other crops along broad river valleys in the northern and eastern parts of this region for centuries. Their land was more fertile than the western plains, with up to 30 inches (76.2 cm) of rainfall a year, tall grasses, and some forested areas. As Native populations increased to the point of straining the resources of these valleys, something occurred that transformed many Native lives. It was the introduction of the horse to America.

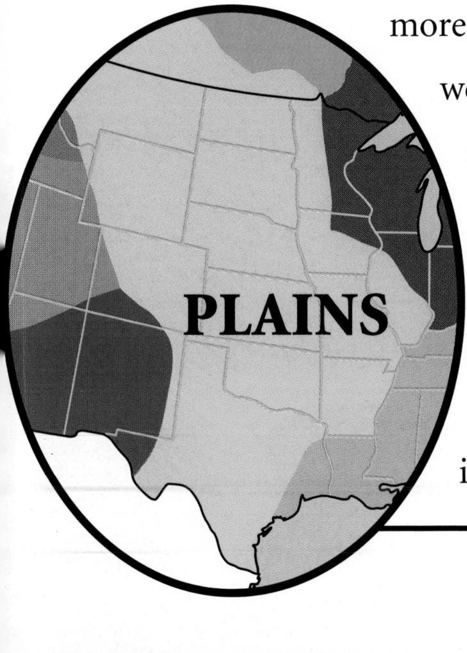

NORTHWEST & SUBARCTIC

PLATEAU

CALIFORNIA

GREAT BASIN

PLAINS

NORTHEAST WOODLANDS

SOUTHWEST

SOUTHEAST WOODLANDS

ATLANTIC OCEAN

PLAINS

The western plains are very dry with natural grasses that once supported huge herds of American **bison** (buffalo). Before the Europeans arrived, more than 50,000,000 bison roamed this region. They traveled in herds of several hundred thousand animals–so large that early explorers reported that the land was covered with buffalo as far as they could see. Many other animals such as antelope, deer, and coyotes, as well as birds, made the plains their home, but the bison was vital to Native life.

Although the early Plains and Prairie Peoples were mainly farmers, they spent several months a year hunting bison. After Spaniards brought horses to Mexico in the 16th century, their use quickly spread to other areas. By 1600, Apache groups in the Southwest were riding horses. Within 100 years, the Plains people had acquired them. They split off from the Prairie groups, abandoned farming, and began to lead a **nomadic** life, following the bison. They could not imagine a time when the great herds that supplied them with everything they needed would no longer exist.

Buffalo still roam the National Bison Range in Montana.

Horses gave people the freedom to travel farther and hunt more efficiently than ever before. Hunters became expert riders, which also made them swift and fearsome warriors. Within a few years another European **import**–firearms–had found its way into the hands of Natives. Horses and guns totally changed Native ways of hunting and fighting.

Although 150 years of conflict and bloodshed between Natives and Europeans were still to come, the earliest contacts were mainly peaceful. In the beginning, traders and trappers arrived in small numbers, and Natives enjoyed trading with them. They traded furs and skins for metal tools, decorative beads, cloth, horses, and guns. In general, they welcomed trading posts in their territory because the presence of traders offered some protection from enemy attacks. However, Natives also obtained liquor at the posts, which had harmful effects on their behavior and morale. Also, traders brought European diseases, to which Natives had no **immunity**. One smallpox outbreak in 1837 spread up the Missouri River by steamship, killing two-thirds of the Blackfeet people, along with thousands of Mandan, Lakota, and Pawnee.

Counting Coup

To a Plains warrior, getting close enough to touch an enemy with the hand, a weapon, or a feather-trimmed stick showed much more courage than attempting to kill him. This was called "counting coup." Warriors boasted about their records; Chief Red Cloud, for instance, had counted more than 80 coup.

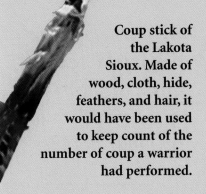

Coup stick of the Lakota Sioux. Made of wood, cloth, hide, feathers, and hair, it would have been used to keep count of the number of coup a warrior had performed.

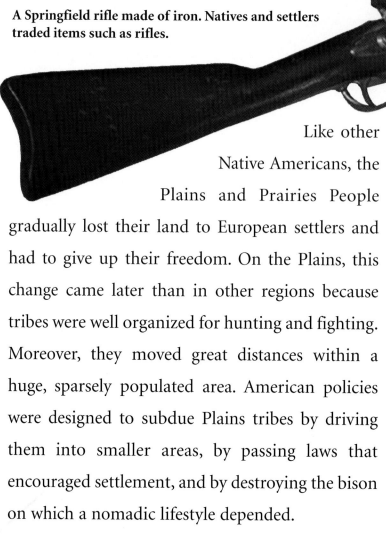

Like other Native Americans, the Plains and Prairies People gradually lost their land to European settlers and had to give up their freedom. On the Plains, this change came later than in other regions because tribes were well organized for hunting and fighting. Moreover, they moved great distances within a huge, sparsely populated area. American policies were designed to subdue Plains tribes by driving them into smaller areas, by passing laws that encouraged settlement, and by destroying the bison on which a nomadic lifestyle depended.

Through **treaties** with U.S. and territorial governments, traditional hunting grounds were surrendered in exchange for government promises of a safe place to live, accompanied by **rations**, money, livestock, and tools. As in other regions, most of the government promises were broken. By the 1840s, about 160,000 Natives remained on the Plains and Prairies, fewer than half of the **pre-Columbian** population.

Plenty Coups

"When the buffalo went away, the hearts of my people fell to the ground, and they could not lift them up again. After this, nothing happened."

–Plenty Coups, a Crow chief

Large numbers of Europeans moving westward in wagon trains spread cholera and other diseases among Natives. They not only killed many antelope and bison for food, but also disrupted the herds' migration. By the 1870s, European Americans were deliberately killing bison to make Native survival more difficult. One bison hunter, William F. "Buffalo Bill" Cody, later boasted that he had personally killed 4,250 bison.

As more and more Europeans passed through, the Plains people turned warlike and raided wagon trains and settlements. To stop these attacks, the U.S. Indian Bureau called a peace council in 1851 in Fort Laramie, Wyoming. Chiefs from a number of tribes signed a treaty, promising not to attack settlers. To discourage intertribal wars, the treaty also defined hunting territories for each group. This was a first step toward forcing the tribes onto reservations.

This mountain of buffalo skulls is only a small part of all the buffalo that had been killed by the mid 1800s.

Little Crow

In 1862, while stealing eggs, some Santee Sioux killed a Minnesota farmer and his family. Chief Little Crow led his people in war against settlers rather than see the young men executed. After dozens of people were killed, the Army sentenced 300 Sioux to hang. President Abraham Lincoln reduced the number to 38. Little Crow was later shot and killed by a farmer, who earned a $75 Indian scalp bounty plus $500 for getting rid of Little Crow.

On the Reservation

Natives on the reservation depended on government supplies of food, clothing, tools, and livestock for survival. But the proud Plains hunters disdained agriculture as "women's work." Some became loggers, laborers, or cowhands. Although they were urged to live in log cabins, in 1900 a third of all Crow still lived in tipis, many pitched next to the homes of relatives.

President Abraham Lincoln

Despite such treaties, conflicts continued. When promised government supplies did not appear, hungry Natives might kill and eat someone's livestock. The Army tended to hold an entire tribe responsible for the deeds of a few. Massacres occurred on both sides, while pressure from hundreds of settlers forced Native groups into smaller and smaller areas.

Natives at first resisted the government's efforts to transform them into farmers. Those who agreed to try farming would cut off their **scalp locks**, a symbol of hunters and warriors. Some converted to Christianity and lived in regular houses, trying to change their ways. Non-reservation Natives, who continued to hunt in their ancient territories and live in **tipis,** called the Native farmers "cut hairs."

Assiniboine camp shows people in front of hide-covered tipis.

One Native leader who tried to cooperate with European Americans was Chief Black Kettle of the Southern Cheyenne. In 1861, he and nine other chiefs signed the Treaty of

Memorial marker of the Sand Creek Massacre

Fort Wise, assuring them a small reservation at Sand Creek, in what is now southeastern Colorado. But some Cheyenne warriors would not observe the treaty and continued to raid, causing Army leaders to plot to get rid of the Cheyenne and their **allies**, the Arapaho [a-rá-pa-ho].

In 1864, 700 troops attacked the peaceful Southern Cheyenne camp at Sand Creek. As Black Kettle gathered his people around an American flag he had treasured, promising that it would protect them, the Army slaughtered more than 400, mostly women and children. Black Kettle and his wife survived, only to be killed four years later when Lt. Col. George Armstrong

Custer led an assault on his camp near Fort Cobb, Oklahoma. Custer, a Civil War veteran, was well known for his exploits against Plains tribes. Later, his name would be forever linked with the Battle of the Bighorn, where Plains People in a brief and shocking hour settled the score.

The only child saved from the Sand Creek Massacre was raised by a woman in Central City. Photo taken in the 1870s

Boarding Schools

The government established off-reservation boarding schools and forced children to attend them. They had to give up their "wild, barbarous ways," which meant cutting their hair, wearing European style clothing, and changing their Native names, languages, and beliefs. Homesick children often ran away, risking beatings, confinement, and humiliation.

Students at the Carlisle School (one of the first off-reservation boarding schools) in Pennsylvania in 1879

In 1867, chiefs of various tribes signed the Medicine Lodge Treaty in Fort Larned, Kansas. It set aside 5,500 square miles (14,244 sq km) of the Indian Territory (Oklahoma) for the Comanche, Kiowa, Kiowa Apache, Cheyenne, and Arapaho. They were to live in houses, raise crops, and give up their nomadic life, including hunting the sacred bison.

The Sioux were some of the last Natives to hold out. They lived in Dakota Territory and ranged westward into the Powder River Country, now eastern Montana and Wyoming. Especially sacred to them was an area known as the Black Hills (in South Dakota), which the Sioux called **Paha-Sapa**. It was the center of their world and the place for seeking visions and spiritual guidance.

Bear Rock is typical of the rock formations in the Black Hills.

The Fetterman Massacre took place near Fort Philip Kearny, Wyoming, in 1866, shown in this illustration.

The chief of the largest group, the Teton or Lakota Sioux, was Red Cloud ("Mahpiua Luta" in Oglala). For years, he kept his people free. He was the only Native leader ever to force the Army to abandon its forts. After steady harassment from Red Cloud's warriors along the Bozeman Trail, Congress withdrew the soldiers, and the Sioux burned down two forts.

The Lakota continued to attack wagon trains and prospectors, trying to keep their hunting grounds intact. But after Crazy Horse, a Lakota chief, led an assault that killed Captain William Fetterman and 80 others, Congress pushed for peace with Red Cloud. In 1868 he signed a treaty, making sure that it defined the Powder River Country as "**unceded** territory" where Indians could hunt "for as long as the buffalo range." Furthermore, the treaty kept the huge Sioux reservation in Dakota Territory undivided.

Red Cloud

Sitting Bull

From an early age, Sitting Bull was strong and generous. He killed his first buffalo calf at age 10 and counted his first coup at age 14. He became a *wichasha wakan* (holy man) who was famous for his speeches.

Crazy Horse

The brilliant Crazy Horse was a holy man but seldom spoke in war councils. Following a boyhood vision, he always went into battle dressed like the warrior of his vision, with lightning painted on his face, marks of hail on his body, and the skin of a red-backed hawk in his hair.

Under the leadership of Chiefs Crazy Horse and Sitting Bull (of the Hunkpapa tribe), a third of the Lakota remained free. But soon the government declared all Natives who refused to live on a reservation "hostile." President Ulysses S. Grant ordered them to report to the agencies by the beginning of 1876, and federal troops began attacking and burning their camps to force them onto reservations.

War ax

Two years earlier, federal troops led by Lt. Col. Custer had found gold in the Black Hills and publicized the discovery widely to break Sioux resistance. By 1881, against all agreements, the great Sioux reservation had been broken into smaller reservations, with many pieces sold to settlers. This came partly as a result of the Battle of the Little Bighorn River, in which Custer and many of his troops were killed.

Lt. Col. Custer

Custer was in charge of the 7th Cavalry under the command of General George Crook. Crook had attacked Sitting Bull's camp on Rosebud Creek in southeastern Montana, killing 30 Sioux and Cheyenne. Sitting Bull moved to the Little Bighorn River (or "Greasy Grass," as the Sioux called it), where he was joined by Natives leaving the reservations to hunt. Soon, more than 4,000 people, including 1,800 warriors, had assembled, the largest Native fighting force ever gathered on the Plains.

Buffalo Calf Woman

At the Battle of the Rosebud, a Cheyenne warrior, Comes in Sight, lost his horse. Facing certain death, he was surprised when a rider raced in, scooped him up, and galloped to safety. Comes in Sight learned later that the rescuer was his sister, Buffalo Calf Woman. Ever since, the Sioux and Cheyenne have called the Battle of the Rosebud "The Battle Where the Girl Saved Her Brother."

Illustration shows the 5th Cavalry at the Battle of the Rosebud.

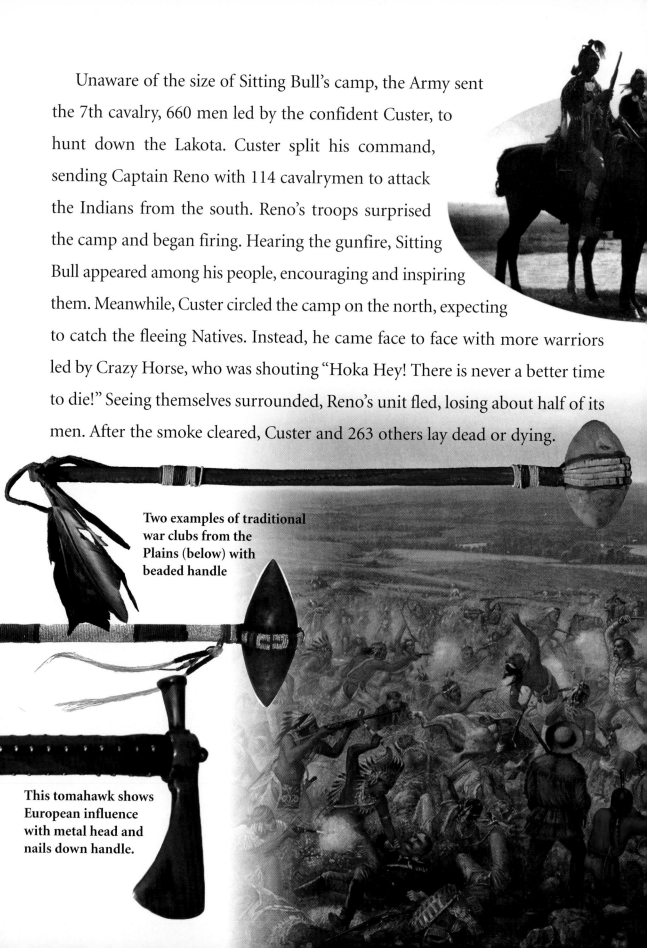

Unaware of the size of Sitting Bull's camp, the Army sent the 7th cavalry, 660 men led by the confident Custer, to hunt down the Lakota. Custer split his command, sending Captain Reno with 114 cavalrymen to attack the Indians from the south. Reno's troops surprised the camp and began firing. Hearing the gunfire, Sitting Bull appeared among his people, encouraging and inspiring them. Meanwhile, Custer circled the camp on the north, expecting to catch the fleeing Natives. Instead, he came face to face with more warriors led by Crazy Horse, who was shouting "Hoka Hey! There is never a better time to die!" Seeing themselves surrounded, Reno's unit fled, losing about half of its men. After the smoke cleared, Custer and 263 others lay dead or dying.

Two examples of traditional war clubs from the Plains (below) with beaded handle

This tomahawk shows European influence with metal head and nails down handle.

When news of the slaughter at the Little Bighorn reached Washington, the nation was stunned. Inquiries and hearings were conducted. Humiliated by Custer's defeat, the Army convinced Congress to put all Indian reservations under its control. A law was passed prohibiting giving supplies or food to the peaceful reservation Sioux as long as their tribesmen roamed free. Within months, the Army began attacking Cheyenne and Sioux camps with large forces. In 1877, Crazy Horse surrendered and led his remaining Oglala and Cheyenne to the Red Cloud Agency in Wyoming. A few months later, he was killed by one of the soldiers sent to imprison him.

Painting by Otto Becker of Custer's Last Stand, the Battle of Little Bighorn. Lt. Col. Custer, wearing buckskin, fights in center.

Government Scouts

The Army enlisted Pawnee, Crow, and Arikara men as scouts to help subdue "hostile Indians." The Indian agencies also recruited Natives to act as agency police, drawing them into bitter disputes with their own people. This ongoing tactic of pitting subgroups against each other is an effective strategy to defeat an entire people.

(Left and right) ceremonial Ghost Dance items

Sitting Bull fled to Canada with his followers. They continued to live freely and hunt buffalo for another four years, but Canada would not give them a reservation, food, or protection from the cold. Finally, in 1881, he and 186 Sioux surrendered. Breaking its promise of a pardon, the Army took Sitting Bull prisoner.

Some years later, a Sioux warrior came to see Sitting Bull with news of a Paiute "messiah" named Wovoka. In a vision, Wovoka had heard a voice commanding him to prepare for the return of all deceased Natives. They would bring back the buffalo, make the Europeans disappear, and renew the world. To prepare for this event, Wovoka founded a religion that required Natives to dance the Ghost Dance.

Painting by Mary Wright of a Ghost Dance circle, 1893

The message of the Ghost Dance spread quickly across reservations, and the desperate Lakota, hungry for hope, adopted it. They added new elements, including a "Ghost Shirt" painted with symbols that were supposed to make the wearer bulletproof. As the dancing spread, Army officers and Indian Bureau agents became alarmed. Fearing that tribes were organizing and reverting to mysterious spiritual practices, the Indian Bureau ordered the Ghost Dance stopped.

(Above) Ghost Dance shirt and (right) Kicking Bear, Chief High Priest of Sioux Ghost Dance in 1896

Although Sitting Bull was skeptical, the Ghost Dance boosted his people's morale so he did not discourage it. But the Indian agent at Standing Rock held Sitting Bull responsible for this new religion. On December 15, 1890, 42 Indian police entered his cabin at the Standing Rock Agency in North Dakota. While he prepared to go with them, some Ghost Dancers tried to stop the police. In the struggle that followed, police rifles were fired and Sitting Bull was killed.

Black Elk and family

*"I can see that something else died there in the bloody mud, and was buried in the blizzard. A people's dream died there. It was a beautiful dream…
the nation's hoop is broken and scattered. There is no center any longer, and the sacred tree is dead."*

–Black Elk, Oglala Sioux, referring to the Battle of Wounded Knee

In 1890, a disastrous event spelled an end to Native American resistance on the Plains. Known as the "Battle of Wounded Knee," it would be more aptly named the "Massacre of Wounded Knee." The remnants of the 7th cavalry pursued Big Foot, a Minneconjou Sioux chief, and 350 followers into the South Dakota Badlands. Caught at their winter camp on Wounded Knee Creek, the band surrendered. One warrior fought for his gun and it went off. The soldiers began shooting at everyone, and the Natives–mostly women and children–ran in panic. Nearly 300 were killed, including Big Foot. Twenty-five soldiers also died, most of them struck by their own bullets or **shrapnel**.

The aftermath of the Battle of Wounded Knee. View to the northeast of Lt. Sydney A. Cloman, 1st Infantry, on his horse. Around him, the frozen bodies of the slain Lakota Sioux lie in the snow of the Pine Ridge Reservation, South Dakota, in 1891.

Despite their disastrous history, the Plains and Prairies People have shown that they are extremely resilient, and they continue to fight for the freedoms they once had. Today they live in houses, drive cars, watch television, and eat many of the same foods that other Americans eat. Children go to public schools and their parents work at a variety of jobs. To maintain the family cooperation and closeness they once had, families still come together for **powwows** and rodeos, and they try to take time to attend these gatherings. For example, the Crow hold an annual fair along the banks of the Little Bighorn River in Montana that features horse racing, traditional dancing, **drumming**, singing, and rodeo competitions.

Wherever they live, Native peoples are interested in preserving their heritage. They make ceremonial clothing, pipes, pouches, **drums**, and other items. They continue to practice their spiritual customs and teach young people tribal languages, songs, dances, and ceremonies. The Sioux are partly responsible for a revived interest in "Indian Culture." For instance, warriors adopted the Grass Dance (in which dancers wore braids of sweetgrass) in the 1860s. The dance of the Omaha, another Siouan tribe, became the basis for the modern powwow in the central and northern Plains.

Lakota Sioux horsehead pipebowl made of red catlinite stone

Senator Campbell on a trip to Kenya, Africa

Sen. Ben Campbell

The only Native American currently in the U.S. Senate is Northern Cheyenne chief Ben Nighthorse Campbell of Colorado. He is the first Native to chair the Indian Affairs Committee. A Korean War veteran, he was a member of the 1964 U.S. Olympic judo team and also is an award-winning jewelry designer. He lost relatives in the Sand Creek Massacre and has recently sponsored legislation making Sand Creek a National Historic Site.

Although the sizes and shapes of reservations have changed over the years, one thing is generally true. Each U.S. reservation has its own government with a **sovereign nation** status. This means that people living there have their own laws and tribal organizations, and in many ways are not subject to U.S. or state laws. For example, reservations have created **casinos** in states where gambling is otherwise illegal. The casinos create jobs and provide money for schools and other programs to raise the standard of living.

Even if their lives will never be what they once were, the Plains and Prairie People have continued to tell their stories. They have produced a number of individuals who have achieved recognition in art, music, film, writing, teaching, and other fields. By listening to their voices, Natives and non-Natives alike can gain greater understanding of who the Plains and Prairies People once were and who they are today.

A Pawnee beaded strip is made of thousands of glass beads sewn onto a hide backing.

Chapter II:

WHERE THEY CAME FROM

BERING STRAIT

Scientists believe that Native Americans descended from Asian people who walked across land or ice bridges beginning perhaps 30,000 years ago. It is also possible that some came by boat. A land **migration** would have occurred at the Bering Strait, a narrow waterway between Siberia (a part of Russia) and the present state of Alaska. Sea levels might have been lower then, exposing land.

Within a few thousand years, descendants of these **immigrants** had spread across North, Central, and South America. They divided into hundreds of different groups, speaking many languages. In some areas, they hunted huge **mammoths** and other great animals that are now extinct. If water was plentiful and they could grow food, they settled down. Over the centuries, many groups migrated from the river valleys onto the plains, hunting bison and living a nomadic life.

Model of mammoth

What Do They Believe about How They Came to America?

The Plains and Prairies People have their own stories about how they originated. Most North American tribes believed that the first parents came either from underground or from the sky.

The Crow believe that Old Man Coyote created the earth. In the beginning, they say, he stood gazing out at an endless sea. He persuaded some ducks to dive down and gather sticks and mud from beneath the water. Coyote's breath transformed them into earth, which he fashioned into mountains, rivers, and canyons. Still lonely, he made men and women, as well as male and female ducks. He met another coyote named Shirape, and together they decided to create other animals, birds, and fish, as well as drums, songs, and dances. Shirape convinced Old Man Coyote to create different languages so there would be war. Without war, he said, you could not have war honors such as wives, gifts, songs, and chiefdom.

Illustration of Old Man Coyote

The Lakota Sioux say that a holy being, White Buffalo Woman, or **Ptesan-Wi**, brought the sacred buffalo calf pipe to the Sioux. Before that, people knew nothing, the sun shone all the time, and there was no game to eat. Ptesan-Wi floated over the prairies in a shining buckskin dress, carrying a sacred bundle, and when she reached the people's camp, she taught them many things. In her bundle was the **chanunpa**, the sacred pipe. She filled it with **chan-shasha**, red willow-bark tobacco. She walked around the lodge four times, symbolizing the circle without end, the sacred hoop of life. The pipe's red bowl, which she held with her left hand, represented the buffalo, as well as the flesh and blood of the red man. The stem, in her right hand, stood for all that grows on the earth. "When the bowl and stem are joined," she said, "it binds men and women together in a circle of love." After giving other gifts, Ptesan-Wi vanished over the horizon and great herds of buffalo appeared, ensuring the people's survival. And the Sioux to this day hold and use the sacred pipe in the ways she taught, and through it communicate with **Wakan Tanka**, the Great Mystery.

According to legend, (above) White Buffalo woman brought the Buffalo, the pipe, and tobacco to the Sioux. (Below) painted buffalo hide

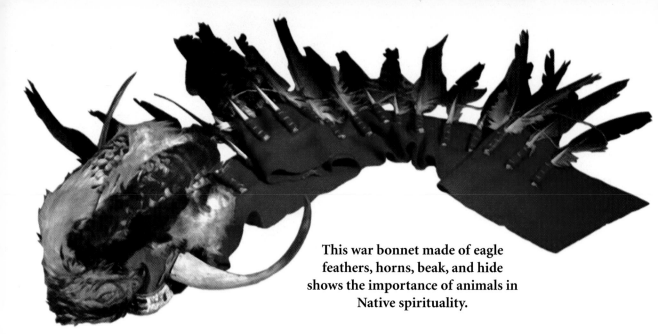

This war bonnet made of eagle feathers, horns, beak, and hide shows the importance of animals in Native spirituality.

According to the Cheyenne, special gifts from Maheo, the Supreme Being—four sacred arrows and a sacred hat—gave their tribe control over animals and enemies alike. They kept these treasures in **medicine bundles**. Two of the arrows were for men and two were for buffalo. The hat, made from the scalp and horns of a buffalo cow, was a guarantee that the buffalo would always continue. Believing that Maheo's power would help them achieve their goals, the Cheyenne carried these bundles into difficult battles or hunting situations.

The creation stories told by a tribe or a nation attempt to explain how people and everything else on Earth came into existence. These are just a few among the countless tales that the Plains and Prairies People pass from generation to generation to make sure that their history, ancient knowledge, and culture survive.

Cheyenne medicine bag

Chapter III:

LIFE ON THE PLAINS & PRAIRIES

The Prairie culture is older than the Plains way of life. Prairie Peoples who lived along rivers grew squash, beans, corn, and other crops and lived in earthen lodges, grouped in villages. They would travel to the bison hunting grounds during the summer and fall. Tribes such as the Dakota Sioux of Minnesota slept in open lodges of poles and bark during the summer, with scaffolds outside for hanging corn and meat to dry.

Semi-permanent Wichita grass house

Man outside Chief Sitting Bull's temporary brush shelter in 1881

(Above) Pawnee speckled corn

Example of a permanent Mandan earthen lodge

Hunting the large and aggressive bison was very dangerous when done on foot, so people worked in groups. Hunters would stampede the herds by setting fire to grass and then herding them over a cliff or into a canyon, where bowmen would shoot as many as they could without getting trampled.

Buffalo

The name "buffalo" came from the word the French explorers gave the shaggy creature, which reminded them of a cow. *Boeuf* [buff] is French for "beef." The American buffalo is a bison, related to the *wisent* (European bison), or wild ox. Both species of bison are extinct in the wild.

Painting of a buffalo hunt from the Acee Blue Eagle Papers

(Above) buffalo hides decorated with feathers, necklace, pipe, and other ornaments

When the horse was introduced, this lifestyle changed dramatically for some Prairie tribes. They gave up farming, or in their words "lost the corn," and followed the bison. They became the Plains Peoples, giving up earthen lodges for the tipi, a house that could be packed up and moved. They used the hides of animals, mainly deer and bison, to make tipis, clothing, and robes or blankets. Moccasins were made of deerskin or bison skin with the fur turned inward. People ate bison meat, used the dung for fuel, and mashed the brains into paste for curing (preserving) the skins. The fat was melted into **tallow** for candles, the hair was braided into ropes, horns were carved into utensils, hoofs were made into rattles, and **tendons** became bowstrings.

Sioux Fighting Style

At the Battle of the Rosebud, Captain Anson Mills described the fighting style of Natives. "In charging toward us [the Indians] exposed little of their person, hanging on with one arm around the neck and one leg over the horse, firing and lancing from underneath the horses' necks so that there was no part of the Indians at which we could aim."

Blackfoot people leading a horse with belongings pulled behind

Plains and Prairies Peoples decorated their clothing and other objects with beautiful sewn or painted designs and long leather fringes. At first they used porcupine quills and shells for decoration, and later beads. They wove bags for gathering food, as well as pouches for carrying tobacco. For ceremonies, people often wore shirts and dresses embellished with elk's teeth, and chiefs had fancy headdresses made of bison skulls with horns. Sometimes, **ermine** pelts or tails were sewn along the sides. The Plains tribes were also famous for their elaborate eagle feather headdresses and war bonnets.

Horses were used as the **dowry** a young man paid for a bride. Giving a large number of horses for a bride meant that a young woman commanded much love and respect from both her family and her future husband.

Although the many tribes of the Plains and Prairies spoke different languages, they traveled widely, trading and visiting. They also intermarried, adopting elements from each other's cultures. If they spoke different languages, people communicated through **sign language**. All of these peoples were adaptable, absorbing new tools and technologies while maintaining their own ancient traditions and beliefs.

This Sioux shirt, made of hide and decorated with paint and fur, shows the decorative dress of Natives of the area.

Caddoan-speaking peoples such as the Pawnee and Arikara lived in the valleys of the Missouri and Platte rivers. They were farming peoples who hunted only in the summer. Other Prairie tribes spoke **Siouan** languages. These included the Hidatsa, Mandan, Omaha, Ponca, Oto, Missouri, and Osage.

Mandan women gathering buffalo berries

The Pawnee were the largest and most notable Prairie tribe. They did not travel far out of fear of their enemies, the Sioux. They wore otter fur turbans and used **cradle boards** decorated with ancient symbols of the sun and morning star. As European settlers moved into the Platte River Valley, they were forced off their land and had to beg food from wagon trains. Some joined the Army and fought the Sioux. Between 1838 and 1880, cholera and smallpox reduced their numbers from 10,000 to about 1,300. Now their population in Oklahoma is about 3,000. Pawnee men and women serving in the Armed Forces are traditionally allowed to return to participate in the Homecoming Powwow held every summer.

A Pawnee cradle board for carrying an infant, made of wood, hide, and buffalo fur

The Plains People

Assiniboine war medicine bag made of hide and beads

Algonkian-speaking Plains tribes include the Cree, the Plains Ojibwe, the Blackfoot, the Gros Ventre ("fat bellies" in French), the Cheyenne ("red talkers"), and the Arapaho ("traders"). In addition, there are Siouan-speaking tribes such as the Assiniboine or Stoney, the various Sioux branches, and the Crow.

More than 20,000 Cree descendants live in the Canadian provinces of Alberta, Saskatchewan, and Manitoba. Several thousand more live on reservations in Montana. About 35,000 Plains Ojibwe live in the same region and in North Dakota.

Cheyenne clowns performing the animal dance

The Blackfoot (or Blackfeet) tribe had three branches, the Northern Blackfoot (Siksika), the Blood, or Kainah, and the Piegan. The Piegan invented the Riding Big or Horse Dance in the 19th century. They painted their horses, decorated them with bells and feathers, and held mock battles, dressed in war regalia. They then danced beside their elegantly attired horses while elders drummed and sang. Today, about 15,000 people live on the Blackfeet Reservation in Montana, where they hold pan-Indian powwows several times a year.

Ancestors of the Cheyenne and Arapaho once lived in earth lodges along the Cheyenne River in present-day North Dakota. After they moved west and became nomadic buffalo hunters, they developed complex spiritual rites. The Cheyenne were early contributors to the ceremony that became known as the Sun Dance. Many Northern Cheyenne live on a reservation in Montana, while the Southern Cheyenne live in Oklahoma. There are about 12,000 total. About 7,000 Arapaho live on reservations in Wind River Wyoming (the northern branch) and Oklahoma (the southern branch).

Horn society pipe bag of the Blackfoot made from hide, beads, sinew, and pigment

The Sioux once lived in present-day southern Minnesota. The eastern groups called all of the Sioux Dakota ("allies"), the middle groups called them Nakota, and the western groups called them Lakota. The word "Sioux" is a French version of an Ojibwe word meaning "adder" or snake. Today there are perhaps 100,000 Sioux in the United States and Canada.

Wounded Knee Siege

On February 27, 1973, armed Natives belonging to the American Indian Movement took over the Wounded Knee Massacre site in the name of the Lakota Nation. They wanted to call attention to conditions on reservations and the violation of treaties. After 71 days, the standoff ended with two Natives dead and several federal agents wounded. The government arrested nearly 1,200 people. Despite their losses, actor Russell Means said, "During the siege at Wounded Knee the American Indians of North America began feeling a resurgence of dignity and pride–an immeasurable benefit that continues to this very day."

The Teton Sioux–which is identical to the Western, or Lakota, division–is the largest of the seven original branches of Sioux. The Teton were the most powerful group of warriors and the last to consent to live on reservations. The Teton Sioux are divided into seven bands, the Hunkpapa, the Oglala, the Sihasapa, and others. About 60,000 Lakota live on various reservations in South Dakota, and a few live in Saskatchewan.

Lakota Sioux woman's necklace made of bone

Medicine Crow of the Apsaroke

Two tribes formed the Middle Sioux, or Nakota–the Yankton and the Yanktonai. They lived along the Missouri River in the 19th century, and today several thousand are mixed with other Sioux in South Dakota and Montana. The Dakota, or Eastern Sioux, are also called the Santee. About 20,000 descendants live on reservations in Nebraska, Minnesota, North Dakota, and in Canada.

The Crow were an important Siouan-speaking tribe that broke into two groups, the River Crow and the Mountain Crow. They lived in present-day Montana and Wyoming. Crow men were among the most impressively dressed of the Plains People, with porcupine quill strips on their arms and shoulders, and an upstanding forelock held in place with bear grease. Most of the 10,000 descendants live on a reservation near Billings, Montana.

Dakota Sioux war dancers

Quanah Parker

One of the last warriors to fight settlers was Quanah Parker. Born in the early 1850s to a Comanche father and a Caucasian mother, he led his band, the Quahada, on raids throughout Texas to avenge his mother's death. As a girl, Cynthia Ann Parker had been kidnapped by Natives but later had lived willingly with the Comanche. Shortly after the Texas Rangers seized Mrs. Parker and her daughter and returned them to her family, both women died. Quanah's father was also killed. In later years, Quanah became a success-ful rancher in Oklahoma. He is known for bringing the **peyote cult** from Mexico and founding the **Native American Church.**

The Comanche speak a **Uto-Aztecan** language. They probably split from the Shoshone in the Great Basin region after obtaining horses and became nomadic. They lived on the southern Plains and were widely feared raiders, attacking other Natives and European settlers alike. Their population fell from about 4,000 in the early 1800s to about 1,500 a century later. It has since risen to about 9,000, although only about 250 people still speak the Comanche language.

The Kiowa ("principal people") speak an independent language related to the **Tanoan** language of the Southwest Pueblo people. They ranged through Montana and the Dakotas and were allies of the Comanche. By the late 1870s, both groups had moved to a reservation in southwest Oklahoma. Now about 12,000 Kiowa live in Caddo County, Oklahoma. They hold powwows and dance the Gourd Dance, which involves rattles and fans.

Painted buffalo skull

Chapter IV:
WHAT THEY BELIEVE

*A*ll Native peoples' calendars, religion, and legends are based on nature. Their lives once depended entirely upon the earth and all that grew on it. To them, everything on Earth has a spiritual purpose and everything is interconnected. Although they may have adapted to new ways and new religions, the old faith remains alive. It is passed from generation to generation through stories and ceremonies.

(Above right) ceremonial circle stick

(Left) the pipe was always offered to the Mystery by holding it aloft. At the feet of the worshipper is a buffalo skull, symbolic of the spirit of the animal which Natives were so dependent on. Pictured is Picket Pin, an Oglala Sioux.

A central belief among Native peoples has to do with the "sacred hoop" or circle. "The Power of the World always works in circles," said Black Elk, a **shaman**, or medicine man, of the Oglala Sioux. He referred not only to physical circles but also to the cycles of life. When seasons change and the stars, planets, sun, and moon seem to move in repeated patterns, it is part of the never-ending circle, also called the **Medicine Wheel**.

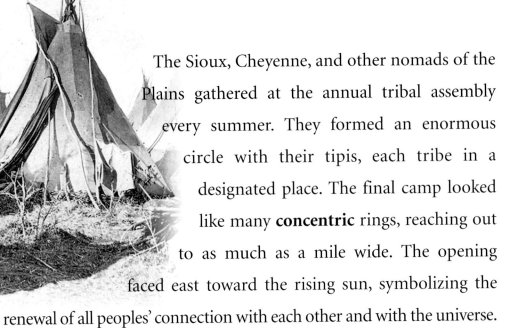

The Sioux, Cheyenne, and other nomads of the Plains gathered at the annual tribal assembly every summer. They formed an enormous circle with their tipis, each tribe in a designated place. The final camp looked like many **concentric** rings, reaching out to as much as a mile wide. The opening faced east toward the rising sun, symbolizing the renewal of all peoples' connection with each other and with the universe.

Also, the Sioux and other Plains tribes dance the Hoop Dance, in which the many spinning hoops symbolize the sun, moon, earth, all light, all life, and the human spirit. The dance shows the interconnection of all things and the hope that someday all peoples will sit together in a great circle of friendship.

Arikara Bear Dance

Sun Dance eagle bone whistle

Ceremonies are important to all Native Americans, but especially to the Plains and Prairies People. The bountiful harvest of bison once made it possible for them to have some leisure time to celebrate. They created elaborate rituals to communicate with the spirit world so their people might live and flourish. The most spectacular ritual was the Sun Dance, which concluded the summer encampment and lasted up to 12 days.

The Plains and Prairie Peoples felt that personal spirits guided them through life. Boys began their **vision quests** very early in life. They walked into the wilderness and stayed alone for a specific number of days–often four, which is considered a sacred number–to receive spiritual power. Some Sioux tribes built a special vision quest site with five wooden poles, four lined up with the four directions and a center pole. Left alone, the seeker would stand at the center pole and cry to Wakan Tanka for a vision, praying to each of the directions as well as to the sky and the earth. The vision usually came in the form of a message or song from an animal or bird.

Sun Dance

At the beginning of each summer encampment, devout Plains warriors joined in the Sun Dance to thank the spirits that guided them. The Lakota offered their flesh and blood as sacrifice to the Great Mystery (Wakan Tanka). The Cheyenne called the Sun Dance the "Lodge of New Birth" while the Crow saw it as a dance of revenge. Today, many Natives still dance the Sun Dance. It sometimes involves cutting a chosen tree, which is carried to the dancing site, or erecting a lodge with a center pole. Dancers gaze at the sun, the tree, or sacred objects on the pole, as they dance for days seeking a vision.

All of the components of ceremonies, such as body paint, drumming, dancing, and vision quests, have to do with spiritual power. Some rituals call upon the cosmic powers to restore harmony and balance on Earth and to protect against misfortune. A person with a lot of spiritual power might become a shaman, or medicine man. In the Plains and Prairies region, shamans are almost always men, although occasionally a woman can be a shaman.

Buffalo Dancer

The Plains and Prairies Peoples once depended on personal spirits to guide them through life. People carried sacred medicine bundles, symbolic objects wrapped in cloth, deerskin, or fur that represented their particular spirit power. Inside the bundle, which was seldom shown to others, might be such items as an eagle's claw, or wolf's tooth, which reflected their owner's dreams and visions. For instance, a warrior who dreamed of water might include a piece of otter skin in his bundle. A tribe or clan might also have such a bundle, symbolizing that group's beliefs about their origins. The Pawnee had an eagle hide stuffed with sacred objects that they believed could be used to bring harm to their enemies.

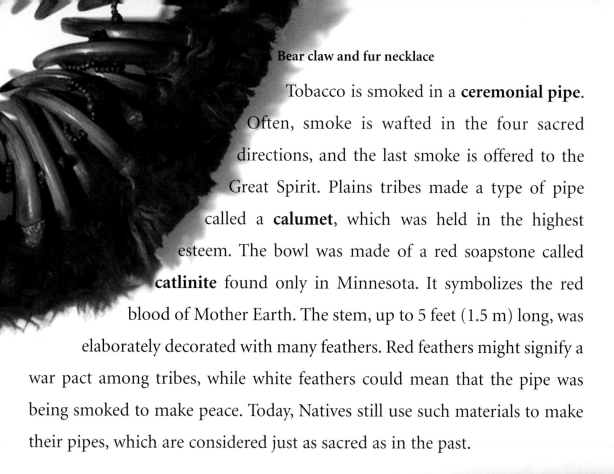

Bear claw and fur necklace

Tobacco is smoked in a **ceremonial pipe**. Often, smoke is wafted in the four sacred directions, and the last smoke is offered to the Great Spirit. Plains tribes made a type of pipe called a **calumet**, which was held in the highest esteem. The bowl was made of a red soapstone called **catlinite** found only in Minnesota. It symbolizes the red blood of Mother Earth. The stem, up to 5 feet (1.5 m) long, was elaborately decorated with many feathers. Red feathers might signify a war pact among tribes, while white feathers could mean that the pipe was being smoked to make peace. Today, Natives still use such materials to make their pipes, which are considered just as sacred as in the past.

Some tribes such as the Crow grew a special tobacco that was never smoked. It was raised only for ceremonial purposes. Members of the Crow Tobacco Society harvested the leaves and held a ceremony to scatter them over a creek or river. The seeds were preserved to plant the next year. This rite celebrated the gift of tobacco and the ties that bind all Crow people together.

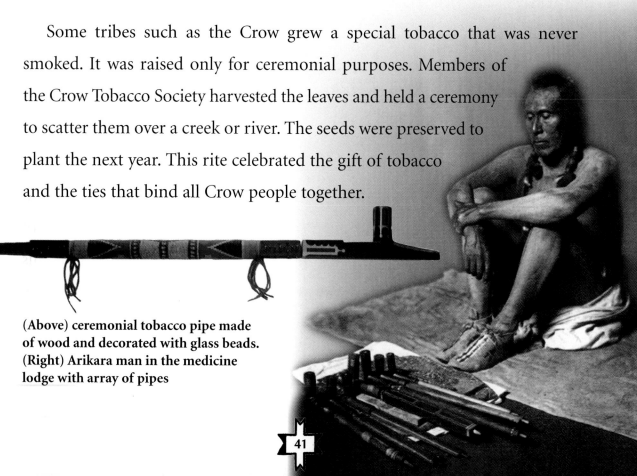

(Above) ceremonial tobacco pipe made of wood and decorated with glass beads. (Right) Arikara man in the medicine lodge with array of pipes

**Bringing the willows
to the sweat lodge**

Another ceremony, a type of community prayer, is the **sweat lodge**. The Sioux call heat and steam **inikagapi**. "Taking a sweat" is a necessary form of purification before major events or ceremonies. Sweating is said to clear away fatigue, distress, and wrong thinking. In early days, dome-shaped sweat lodges were made of buffalo hides stretched over bent willows.

Drums and drumming represent the pulse of the universe, as well as the human heartbeat. Each drum is considered a sacred object and has a drum-keeper to protect it from casual use. Dances began as ways to tell the story of a hunt or battle. Both men and women still dance traditional dances.

Sacred clowns, or "contraries," are an important part of Plains ceremonies. People become clowns (**heyoka** in the Sioux language or **hohnuhk'e** in Cheyenne) after having a dream or vision of thunder and lightning. They do everything in reverse. For instance, they sit on their horses backwards, come closer when told to leave, and say no when they mean yes. The Sioux believe that contraries are related to the **Wakinyan** (thunderbird) and that they bring messages. They also put people in a happy frame of mind to prepare for a great truth, such as a decision to make war or peace.

(Above) traditional Blackfoot war club, (right) traditional Sioux war bonnet, and (below) Iron horse, Natives' name for the railroad, was a major factor in the destruction of the traditional way of life for the Plains Indians.

Early peoples could not understand the European view that the earth is something that can be bought and sold. When European-Americans slaughtered the bison from trains or from horses and left them to rot, Natives watched with astonishment. When settlers cut down forests for houses, plowed up the earth to plant crops, and fenced off the land to keep others out, Natives were shocked. These actions struck deeply at their belief that the earth is sacred. Today, Native people across the continent are committed to healing the damage that civilization has caused to the natural environment.

Once, the survival of Native tribes depended on having strong and brave warriors, and warriors' deeds were honored through ceremonies. Today, that feeling is kept alive in the respect shown to veterans of U.S. wars. Large numbers of Native men and women have served in the Armed Forces and have fought in every war. Veterans are honored for their willingness to die for their country. Today, powwows and tribal ceremonies often include **flag songs** and similar observances for Native veterans.

A TIMELINE OF THE HISTORY OF THE PLAINS & PRAIRIES PEOPLE

30,000 to 13,000 BC - Ice ages lower sea levels, making it possible for people to walk across a land bridge from Asia to North America.

12,000 to 9,000 BC - Earth warms up and ice caps melt, allowing people to move throughout the Americas.

AD 1492 - Christopher Columbus arrives in America. Thinking he is in India, he names the inhabitants "Indians."

AD 1630s - Northern Prairie groups are trading furs with the French.

AD 1700 - Plains groups begin to acquire horses, moving to the more arid regions and following the buffalo.

AD 1776 to 1783 - The American Revolution is fought and creates a new country, the United States of America.

AD 1803 - United States buys Louisiana Territory from France for $15 million, doubling the size of the country.

AD 1830 - Passage of Indian Removal Act.

AD 1849 - Gold discovered in California, prompting a rush of settlers across the Plains.

AD 1862 - The Homestead Act promises farmers free land for cultivation in the thinly populated central United States.

AD 1864 - Sand Creek Massacre of Black Kettle's Southern Cheyenne.

AD 1861 to 1865 - The American Civil War is fought and ends with the abolition of slavery.

AD 1867 - Medicine Lodge Treaty signed at Fort Larned, Kansas, sending groups of Plains People to Indian Territory (Oklahoma).

AD 1869 - The first transcontinental railroad is finished.

AD 1876 - Battle of the Little Big Horn, in which the Sioux kill Lt. Col. George Armstrong Custer and most of his troops.

AD 1890 - Wounded Knee Massacre.

AD 1973 - Members of Lakota and other tribes occupy Wounded Knee site for 71 days.

GLOSSARY

Algonkian - A family of Native American languages spoken from Labrador to Carolina and westward into the Great Plains.

ally - A person or group that associates with another to promote common interests.

American Indian - A member of the first peoples of North America.

bison - One of two species of wild oxen, the European bison and the American bison.

Caddoan - A family of Native American languages spoken on the southern Plains.

calumet - A ceremonial pipe made by Native Americans with a bowl of red stone and a long reed for a stem.

casino - A building used for gambling.

catlinite - A red soapstone found only in Minnesota and named after George Catlin.

ceremonial pipe - A device for smoking sacred substances, such as tobacco, during a formal event or for an official purpose.

chan-shasha - Red willow bark; Lakota.

chanunpa - Lakota word for sacred pipe.

concentric - Having a common center, such as circles that are drawn one inside the other.

cradle board - A woven or sewn pouch attached to a stiffer frame made of wood or reeds for holding an infant securely.

dance - A series of rhythmic movements, often performed to music.

dowry - The money, goods, or estate that a woman brings her husband in marriage.

drum - A hollow instrument with coverings, such as skins, over the ends.

drumming - Making a series of strokes or vibrations that produce rhythmic sounds.

ermine - A type of weasel with a coat that turns white in winter, with a black-tipped tail.

flag songs - Songs performed at gatherings, usually on Veteran's Day, that developed from ancient ceremonies honoring Native warriors.

heyoka - Sacred clowns in Siouan.

hohnuhk'e - Cheyenne for sacred clowns.

immigrant - A person who comes to a country to live in it.

immunity - Ability to resist disease.

import - Something moved into one country or region from another for the purposes of trade.

inikagapi - Heat/steam in the Siouan language.

mammoth - Extinct hairy elephants living about 1,600,000 years ago.

medicine bundle - A collection of animal parts and other objects believed to possess sacred meaning or magical powers.

Medicine Wheel - The concept that the "power of the world" moves in a circle.

migration - The movement of a person or group from one country or place to another.

Native American - A synonym for American Indian.

Native American Church - A Native religion founded in 1918 in Oklahoma, which features the use of peyote for spiritual renewal and requires people to abstain from alcohol.

nomadic - Refers to people who move from place to place, usually in relation to the seasons and food supply, and have no fixed residence.

Paha-Sapa - Lakota word for "black hills."

peyote cult - A Native religion, brought from Mexico, that includes eating the center bud of a small cactus, also called "mescal," which helps bring visions.

Plains and Prairie People - The Natives of a vast region west of the Mississippi River.

powwow - Originally referred to a shaman, a vision, or a gathering. Now, it means a cultural, social, and spiritual gathering to celebrate Native culture and pride.

pre-Columbian - Referring to the time before Christopher Columbus arrived in America.

Ptesan-Wi - White Buffalo Woman.

ration - Allowance of food or other supplies.

reservation - A tract of public land set aside for a specific use. Tracts set aside for Natives. In Canada, they are called "reserves."

scalp lock - The bunch of hair that remained on top of a warrior's head after he had shaved off the rest.

shaman - Medicine man or woman.

shrapnel - Fragments of exploded bombs or shells.

sign language - A formal language that uses hand gestures instead of words.

Siouan - A family of Native American languages that is the main language family on the Plains.

sovereign nation - A community of people that has independent power and freedom.

sweat lodge - A small building used for communal prayer and purification by sweating.

tallow - The white, odorless fat of cattle or sheep that has been melted and solidified.

Tanoan - A family of Native American languages spoken along the Rio Grande River valley in New Mexico.

tendon - A tough cord or band of tissue that connects a muscle with some other part, such as bone.

tipi - A conical tent made of poles and skins.

treaty - An agreement or arrangement, usually written, made by negotiating.

unceded - Something not yielded or given up.

Uto-Aztecan - A family of Native American languages created by merging a Mexican language family (Aztecan) with the Shoshonean family of the western U.S.

vision quest - The seeking of a vision, dream, or perception, which will guide a young person for life.

Wakan Tanka - Lakota word for "the Great Mystery."

Wakinyan - Siouan word for thunderbird.

Books of Interest

Bruchac, Joseph. *A Boy Called Slow: The True Story of Sitting Bull.* Glenview, Ill.: Scott Foresman (paperback ed.), 1994.

Erdoes, Richard and Alfonso Ortiz, eds. *American Indian Myths and Legends.* New York: Pantheon, 1984.

Erlich, Amy, adapter. *Wounded Knee: An Indian History of the American West.* New York: Henry Holt & Co. 1993 (adaptation for young readers of Dee Brown's *Bury My Heart at Wounded Knee,* Henry Holt & Co., 1970).

Johnson, Michael. *Encyclopedia of Native Tribes of North America.* New York: Gramercy Books, 2001.

Neihardt, John G. *Black Elk Speaks.* New York: Bison Books Corp. (paperback ed.), 2000.

Nerburn, Kent, ed. *The Wisdom of the Native Americans.* Novato, Calif.: New World Library, 1999.

Wood, Ted. *A Boy Becomes a Man at Wounded Knee.* New York: Walker & Co., 1992.

Woodhead, Henry, series ed. *The American Indians.* Alexandria, Va.: Time Life Inc., 1992-94.

Children's Atlas of Native Americans. Chicago: Rand McNally & Co., 1996.

Good Web Sites to Begin Researching Native Americans

General Information Site with Links
http://www.nativeculture.com

Resources for Indigenous Cultures around the World
http://www.nativeweb.org/

Index of Native American Resources on the Internet
http://www.hanksville.org/NAresources/

News and Information from a Native American Perspective
http://www.indianz.com

An Online Newsletter Celebrating Native America
http://www.turtletrack.org

Native American History in the United States
http://web.uccs.edu/~history/index/nativeam.html

Internet School Library Media Center
http://falcon.jmu.edu/~ramseyil/native.htm

INDEX

Linda Thompson is a Montana native and a graduate of the University of Washington. She has been a teacher, writer, and editor in the San Francisco Bay Area for 30 years and now lives in Taos, New Mexico. She can be contacted through her web site, http://www.highmesaproductions.com